The Fall of the House of Usher

and Other Stories

EDGAR ALLAN POE

Level 3

Retold by Adrian Kelly
Series Editors: Andy Hopkins and Jocelyn Potter

D0978107

Pearson Education Limited
Edinburgh Gate, Harlow,
Essex CM20 2JE, England
and Associated Companies throughout the world.

ISBN-13: 978-0-582-42128-8
ISBN-10: 0-582-42128-4

This selection of stories first published 2000

7 9 10 8 6

Text copyright © Penguin Books 2000
Illustrations copyright © George Sharp (Virgil Pomfret) 2000

Typeset by Digital Type, London
Set in 11/14pt Bembo
Printed in China
SWTC/06

Published by Pearson Education Limited in association with
Penguin Books Ltd, both companies being subsidiaries of Pearson Plc

For a complete list of titles available in the Penguin Readers series please write to your local
Pearson Education office or contact: Penguin Readers Marketing Department,
Pearson Education, Edinburgh Gate, Harlow, Essex, CM20 2JE.

Contents

Introduction

After a few days, my friend looked better, but then he began to act strangely and nervously again. He seemed to have a terrible secret. His skin became paler, and he looked into empty space for hours. He seemed to listen for a sound. He scared me. I thought that he was, now, going completely mad.

"The Fall of the House of Usher" is one of Edgar Allan Poe's most famous short stories. It is the story of a strange house and its even stranger owners, Roderick Usher and his sister, Madeline. The house, Usher believes, is making him and his sister sick. They are going mad. He writes a letter to an old friend, and asks him for help. But can the friend really help? Can Usher win the fight against his madness? And will Madeline ever be well again?

In "The Barrel of Amontillado," another famous short story, we meet a second madman, Montresor. A friend has said and done terrible things to him. But he receives a punishment that is much, much worse. "The Maelström" describes the fear of death during a wild storm on the ocean.

In "The Murders of the Rue Morgue" and "The Stolen Letter," we meet C. Auguste Dupin, Poe's famous Parisian detective. Poe is known as one of the fathers of the detective story, and Dupin is a very clever and interesting man. He solves problems that are mysteries to the local police.

Poe's stories are still popular 150 years after his death. As you read them, you will understand this. Dupin can see into people's hearts and minds. Poe can too.

Edgar Allan Poe was born in Boston, Massachusetts, in 1809, and died in Baltimore, Maryland, in 1849. His parents were traveling actors. Before Poe was two years old, both of his parents died.

John Allan, a Virginia businessman, and his wife agreed to look after young Poe. From 1815 to 1820, Poe lived in England with the Allans.

As Poe grew older, he and Allan disagreed about many things. Poe studied for a short time at the University of Virginia. But he had to leave school because Allan refused to give him enough money.

In 1827 Poe wrote his first book of poems, *Tamerlane and Other Poems*. Soon after that, he became a soldier, using the name of Edgar A. Perry. He continued to write, and in 1829 his second book of poems, *Al Aaraaf*, came out.

In 1930 Allan helped Poe go to West Point, the famous school for soldiers, but Poe was later asked to leave. He did not mind, because he did not like the school or Allan's plans for him. He wanted to write. In 1831, he wrote his third book, *Poems*.

Most of Poe's early work did not become famous. So he worked for newspapers to earn a little money. He moved to Baltimore and lived there with his aunt, Mrs. Clemm. He lived with her for a number of years, and then in 1836 he married her daughter, his cousin, Virginia. She was only fourteen. At this time Poe also began to write short stories for magazines. His first book of stories, *Tales of the Grotesque and Arabesque*, came out in 1839.

In 1845 Poe became well known for *The Raven and Other Poems*. He was almost always poor, though, and he was not often happy. Poe's life was sometimes similar to his writing. He drank a lot and, like Roderick Usher and many of the people in his stories, he often fought with madness. When his wife died, in 1847, he drank more. All his life he suffered from illnesses, of the body and the mind.

Poe did not live a long life, and it was a sad death. Many later writers, though, spoke very well of him. He was, they knew, very important to literature. The famous French writer, Baudelaire, liked Poe's work very much, and wrote many of his stories and poems in French. The English writers Algernon Charles Swinburne and Oscar Wilde, and the Irish poet William Butler Yeats, also enjoyed Poe's work. "Poe was a great writer to all people for all time," Yeats said. Sigmund Freud was very interested in the way that Poe saw the dark side of the mind.

Today, Poe is known as one of the best early writers of scary stories, and of detective stories or murder mysteries. Famous writers like Stephen King and Clive Barker say that Poe was their greatest teacher.

The Fall of the House of Usher

On a dark, silent day in fall I was riding alone through flat, gray countryside. As evening came, I first saw the melancholy House of Usher.

Immediately, I felt a terrible sadness. The house was dark, with windows like empty eyes. Almost nothing grew in the grounds around it. My heart felt cold, like ice; I was afraid.

I stopped to think. Why did the house make me so uncomfortable? It was a mystery. We cannot always understand why some things scare us. But I had to continue toward the dark house, because I was planning to stay there for a few weeks.

The owner of the house, Roderick Usher, was a close friend when I was a boy. I heard nothing from him for many years, until he wrote me a letter.

The letter was very strange. In it, he asked me to come and see him. He was very sick, he said, in body and in mind. Only a visit from me, his best and only friend, could help to make him well and happy again. His request seemed to come from his heart, and I could not say no.

Usher and I were very good friends as children, but I did not know much about him. He always disliked being around people. The Ushers were not like other people. They loved art and music. They were very rich, and gave money away to poorer people, but they were also very private. Because the same house was always passed down from father to son, people called the family, too, the "House of Usher."

I looked again at the house, and at the grounds around it. Again I felt afraid. The air seemed to hang over the house and grounds, and it smelled of death.

"I am dreaming," I thought. "I am making myself afraid."

The house was very old, and in a terrible state.

I shook my head, and looked again. The house was very old, and in a terrible state. Looking closely, I noticed a narrow crack in the wall. It began at the roof and made its way down the side of the house.

I crossed a bridge to the house. A man was waiting for me on the other side, and he took my horse. I went into the house, and another man took me through it. He did not say a word. Each room was very dark.

I felt as uncomfortable inside the house as outside. Even ordinary furniture looked strange. Then, near a stairway, I met the family doctor. He, too, acted strangely. He said hello nervously, but walked quickly away.

At last my guide took me to the door of Roderick Usher's room, and let me in.

It was difficult to see the room because there was little light. It seemed very large, though, with a black, wooden floor. The furniture was old, and looked uncomfortable. Books were everywhere, but they brought no life to the room. The air was heavy with sadness.

Then I saw Usher. He was lying on a sofa, but he got up and said hello to me warmly. But was it really him? When we sat down, I could not believe it.

He was a good looking boy, all those years ago. His face was thin but handsome, his eyes shone, and his hair was soft and beautiful. Now his hair was thin and wild, his eyes were large and wet, and his face was terribly pale. I felt sorry for him.

My friend was acting as strangely as he looked. One minute he was excited and happy, and spoke very quickly. The next minute he was sad, and spoke very slowly.

He was glad to see me, he said. He hoped that I could help him, and his illness.

He believed that this illness was in his family. It attacked his senses, he said. He could eat only simple foods, and wear only soft clothes. Weak light hurt his eyes, and even flowers smelled bad to him. Music was the only sound that pleased him. He was always afraid.

"I will die," he said. "I *must* die if this illness continues. I fear the future. I fear that I will lose my mind completely. I am afraid that I will die of fear."

Usher never left the house. But he believed that the house was the reason for his strange illness. His dear sister, Madeline, was suffering from a similar illness. She was dying, and was Usher's last living relative.

"When she dies," he said, "I will be the last of the Ushers."

While he spoke, the lady Madeline suddenly came into the room. She passed through it without noticing me. She seemed so strange, and not of this earth. Looking at her, I was afraid again. My friend cried when he saw her.

Madeline's illness was a mystery to the family doctor. She was not interested in anything, and she was dying like a flower without water. She was growing weaker every day.

The next day she did not leave her bed. Maybe I have seen her, I thought, for the first and last time.

Madeline's name was not spoken for days as I tried to help my friend. We painted and read together, or I listened patiently to Usher's strange songs.

I soon realized, though, that I could not help his melancholy. His books, his songs, and his pictures showed me the state of his mind. One of his pictures was of a very long, brightly lit white tomb deep in the earth. I will never forget it, and the many strange hours that I spent with him.

Then, one evening, Usher told me suddenly of the lady Madeline's death. He wanted to place her body in one of the many tombs under the house. I agreed to help him put the body there.

She seemed so strange, and not of this earth.

The tomb, I soon learned, was below my bedroom. It was very small, and completely dark. Its walls were wet, and it smelled of death. When we opened the door, it grated loudly. I was glad that it was made of thick, heavy metal.

We put Madeline in her tomb. Then Usher and I stopped and looked at her face.

"Look," said Usher. "In death her face has more color. Does she not seem to smile?"

He was right. In death her face seemed more alive. We could not look at the dead lady for long, though, and soon returned upstairs.

After a few days, my friend looked better, but then he began to act strangely and nervously again. He seemed to have a terrible secret. His skin became paler, and he looked into empty space for hours. He seemed to listen for a sound. He scared me. I thought that he was, now, going completely mad.

Late one night, seven or eight days after we put Madeline in her tomb, I could not sleep. Outside, there was a terrible storm, and the wind crashed against my windows. Then, between the noises of the storm, I thought that I heard low, heavy, mysterious sounds. I was afraid. I got up quickly, put on my clothes, and began walking around my room.

I heard steps outside my door, then a knock. It was Usher. He was as white as a sheet, and was laughing like a madman. But I let him in because I was so afraid.

He looked around in silence, then said, "Have you seen it? Wait—you will, you will."

He hurried to one of the bedroom's large windows, and opened it wide. The wind and rain came in. The storm was unnaturally strong, and there was a strange light around the house.

"You must not look at this!" I said to Usher, taking him away from the window to a chair. "Let's close the window. The air is

6

cold, and dangerous to your health. Here, sit, and I shall read you one of your favorite stories. We will spend this terrible night together."

I picked up a book that told the story of Ethelred. It was not Usher's favorite story—it was just the nearest book. Usually Usher did not like stories that were too simple for his intelligent mind. I hoped, though, that I could calm him with an old story about a brave man.

I began to read, and Usher seemed to be very excited by the story. I came to the part where Ethelred tries to get into the house of a crazy old man. The man lives alone in the forest. Ethelred asks to come in, but the old man refuses. The story goes like this:

"The old man refused to let Ethelred in. But a terrible storm was beginning, and Ethelred could not wait. He was strong and brave, and he lifted his heavy stick. He began to hit the door, and to break it down. The noise was loud and traveled all over the forest."

At the end of this sentence, I stopped in fear.

I thought I heard a sound from somewhere in the house. Or was it the storm outside? I continued to read.

"When Ethelred got through the door, he did not see the crazy old man. To his surprise, there was a large and terrible animal in the man's place. It was like no animal on earth. Next to it was a pile of gold. On the wall above it was a metal sign that read, 'You are here, so you are brave. If you kill the animal, you will win the gold.'

"Ethelred lifted up his stick and hit the animal on the head. It fell down, and died. But before it died, it screamed. The noise was loud and terrible, and Ethelred had to cover his ears."

Again, I stopped reading. I was sure that I heard a long screaming sound. The sound was not in my mind, from the story.

It came from inside the house. I said nothing, though, because I did not want to excite Usher. Could he hear the sounds too? I was not sure, so I continued to read.

"After Ethelred killed the animal, the metal sign on the wall fell to the floor with a loud ringing sound."

As I read the words "ringing sound," I heard a similar sound inside the house. I felt terrible fear. This time I was sure. Someone was screaming, and hitting metal.

Then I heard grating sounds. A heavy metal door was opening.

I knew now that Usher was listening to the sounds too. The look on his face was different. He turned his chair and faced the door of the room. His eyes were open wide, and his body was shaking. He began to talk to himself in a low voice.

I jumped to my feet and ran to Usher. He was looking straight in front of him, and did not notice me. When I put my hand on his shoulder, he shook again. Then he spoke words that I will never forget.

"*Now* do you hear it? *I* hear it, and *have* heard it. I have heard it for many minutes, many hours, and many days, but I could not speak. Now I am telling you. *She was alive when we put her in the tomb!* Will she be here soon? Is she coming to punish me? Can I hear her feet on the stairs? Can I hear the sound of her *heart*?" He jumped to his feet. "*Madman! I am telling you that she is just outside the door!*"

Suddenly the door of the room opened, and there stood the lady Madeline. There was blood on her white clothes, and her body was terribly thin. For a few seconds she stood in the doorway, shaking. Then, she fell toward her brother, with a cry. As they crashed heavily to the floor, they both died.

I ran from the room, and from the house. Outside, the storm was still crashing against the building. On the bridge, I turned and looked behind me. The crack in the wall of the house was

Suddenly the door of the room opened . . .

getting wider. Through it, I could see the full, blood-red moon. Then a great wind came. I watched in fear as the house fell in pieces to the ground. The House of Usher was destroyed.

The Maelström

We finally reached the top of the highest mountain. For some minutes, the old man seemed too tired to speak.

"Not long ago," he said at last, "I guided people up this mountain. But about three years ago, a terrible thing happened to me. No living person has seen anything like it. My body and my mind were broken by the six hours of terrible fear that I went through that day.

You believe that I am a *very* old man. I am not. In less than a day, my hair changed from black to white. My body became weak. Walking makes me shake. A shadow now scares me. I feel nervous when I am on this little mountain. Did you know that?"

The "little mountain" was about five hundred meters high. *I* was nervous. Below us, the mountain fell away in a straight wall of black shining rock. I fell to the ground in fear. For a few minutes I could not look up at the sky or out at the sea.

"You must not be afraid," said my guide. "Here is the best view of the place where my story happened. That is why I have brought you here."

"We are now," he continued, "close to the coast of Norway, in the area called Lofoden. This mountain is called Helseggen, the Cloudy. Now, stand up, and look out to sea."

I did as he asked. Ten or twelve kilometers away, I could see a small, empty island. The waves crashed against it. About four kilometers closer, there was a smaller island. This was also empty, and it had dark rocks all around it.

"The far island is called Vurggh by the Norwegians," said the old man. "The closer one is called Moskoe."

The water between the two islands looked very unusual. There was a strong wind from the sea, but the waves did not move with the wind. They moved everywhere, quickly and angrily, sometimes against the wind.

"Tell me," continued the old man, "can you hear anything? Can you see a change in the water?"

When the old man spoke, I began to hear a loud sound. At the same time, I saw that the ocean *was* changing. It was becoming rough, and was beginning to move even more quickly. With each second, it moved faster. In five minutes the sea between Vurggh and the mountain was turning in terrible whirlpools. Between Moskoe and the coast, it turned most wildly.

"Have you ever seen anything like it?" asked the old man.

I could say nothing as I watched. In a few minutes the small whirlpools suddenly became one. It was more than a kilometer wide. The great whirlpool's walls were smooth and black. They turned with great speed. The whirlpool made a screaming sound, like no other sound on earth. The mountain shook under our feet. I threw myself to the ground again in fear.

"*This*," I said at last to the old man, "this is the great whirlpool of the Maelström."

"It is sometimes called that," he said. "We Norwegians call it the Moskoe-ström."

I knew about the whirlpool, but I could not believe my eyes.

"Have a good look," said the old man, "and then listen to my story."

I did what he asked.

"I and my two brothers," he began, "owned a large fishing boat. We fished around the islands of Moskoe and Vurggh. It is dangerous, but there are a lot of fish in those waters.

"Usually we waited for good weather and the turn of the tide. At the turn of the tide, the Moskoe-ström is calm for fifteen minutes. When it was calm, we sailed across. Then we fished for the day and returned at the next turn of the tide. We always

The whirlpool made a screaming sound, like no other sound on earth.

waited for a good wind so we could sail quickly. We were almost caught by the whirlpool only twice in six years. We were always careful, but it *was* a terrible danger.

"Then, almost three years ago, there was a storm which the people here will never forget. The weather that morning and afternoon was fine. The sun shone, and the wind came softly from the southwest. Even the oldest sailor did not see that a storm was coming.

"My brothers and I sailed to the islands at about two o'clock in the afternoon. We caught more fish that day than ever before. It was seven by my watch when we started for home. We wanted to cross the Ström at eight o'clock, when it was calm.

"We never dreamed of danger, because the weather seemed so good. Then the wind suddenly changed, and became very strong. I looked behind me.

"The sky was covered by a great storm cloud. In less than a minute the storm reached us, and in less than two minutes the sky was completely black. Because of the darkness and the heavy rain, I could not see my brothers in the boat. It was terrible. Nobody in Norway remembers a storm like it.

"Almost immediately, my younger brother was knocked into the water by the wind. I could not think. In my fear, I lay down and held onto a metal ring in the bottom of the boat. For a few seconds we were completely covered in water.

"Then I felt somebody holding onto my arm. It was my older brother. I was happy that he was alive. But my happiness soon disappeared. He put his mouth close to my ear and screamed, '*the Moskoe-ström!*'

"I shook from head to foot. We were going into the whirlpool and nothing could save us. A terrible thought came to me. I took my watch out of my pocket. It was not going. *It still said seven o'clock*. The whirlpool was now as strong as it ever got. And the wind was taking us straight toward it!

The wind was taking us straight toward it!

"Two minutes later, we were close to the whirlpool's mouth. We went round and round it for about an hour. Each time, our boat went closer to the terrible mouth. When I was so close to death, my fear left me. I had no hope now, and I became almost calm. I began to think that this was a good way to die. You can believe me or not, but I *wanted* to see the inside of the whirlpool.

"My brother did not feel the same way. When we came close to the whirlpool, he attacked me like a madman. He was very scared, and wanted to hold onto the metal ring. I left it for him, because it could not save us. I went to the back of the boat and held onto a water barrel.

"Seconds later, the boat was swept into the whirlpool. We fell, and I closed my eyes. I was ready to die immediately.

"Seconds passed. I was still alive!

"I opened my eyes. I will never forget what I saw. It was wonderful and terrible at the same time. The boat seemed to *hang* on the inside of the whirlpool. The sides of the whirlpool were perfectly smooth, black, and shining with moonlight.

"The moonlight reached the bottom of the whirlpool, and I saw a rainbow there. It was like a bridge between this world and the next world. But the noise of the whirlpool was a terrible scream.

"The boat went round and round. It was going down and down, toward the bottom where the waters crashed together. But our movement was very slow, so I had time. I looked around me.

"Our boat was not the only thing that was caught in the whirlpool. Above and below us I saw pieces of other boats, broken boxes, trees, and barrels. I tried to guess: 'Which things will fall the fastest?' I was wrong every time. Lighter things did not fall faster than heavier ones.

"I thought about this. Suddenly, I was full of new hope. I realized that, at the turn of the tide, smaller things went up to the sea again. Barrels, I saw, were falling very slowly.

"I decided quickly. I tied myself to the water barrel. I tried to explain my plan to my brother. At last he understood, but he was too afraid to move. There was no more time. I said goodbye to him, and jumped into the water.

"An hour later, I watched the boat crash into the bottom of the pool. But I, on my barrel, did not fall far. Then, at last, the whirlpool began to calm, and I began to move up. Soon, I was in the place where the Moskoe-ström *was*. The sea was still stormy, but luckily it carried me to the calm fishing grounds. There, a boat found me and took me out of the water.

"At first, I could not speak. The fishermen on the boat were my old friends, but they did not know me. I was a stranger to them. My black hair was white, and my face was completely changed too. When I told them my story, they did not believe me. Do you?"

The Barrel of Amontillado*

I knew a man who was named Fortunato. I called him my friend, but truly I hated him. He did and said many terrible things to me. I decided to punish him. I promised myself. But I was patient, and did not tell anyone about my promise.

I wanted to punish him very much, but I did not want anyone to catch me. If you are caught, a wrong is not made right. It is also important that the other person *knows*. He must know who is punishing him.

Fortunato always believed that I liked him. My words and actions showed that I was a friend. I always smiled at him. I was smiling because I was thinking of his death. But he, of course, did not know that.

All men have weak points, and Fortunato's weakness was wine. He loved it. He did not know much about any other subject, but he knew a lot about wines. I also liked wine and knew a lot about it. I bought large amounts of it when I could.

Every year, the city had a big party. One evening at this time, I met Fortunato in the street. He said hello very warmly. He was wearing a party hat and colorful clothes, and he was quite drunk. I shook his hand for a long time because I was *very* pleased to see him.

I said, "My dear Fortunato! You look very well today! I am lucky to meet you! I have bought a barrel of wine. I think that it is Amontillado. But I am not sure."

"What?" he said. "Amontillado? *You* bought a barrel of Amontillado? At this time of year? It is not possible!"

"Maybe you are right," I answered. "I was very silly, and I paid

---

* Amontillado: a special type of wine.

18

the full price for it too. I wanted to ask you about it first, but I could not find you. I really wanted to buy the Amontillado before another man took it."

"Amontillado!"

"I think it is Amontillado."

"Amontillado!"

"I must be sure, though."

"Amontillado!"

"I can see that you are busy. So I am on my way to talk to Luchesi. He knows wine *very* well. He will be able to tell me if it is Amontillado."

"Luchesi cannot tell the difference between Amontillado and water."

"But many people say that he knows as much about wine as you."

"Come. Let's go."

"Where to?"

"To your house."

"My friend, no. You are too kind. It is easy to see that you are busy. I will go to Luchesi."

"I am not busy. Let's go."

"But my friend, you seem to have a very bad cough. I keep my wine in the caves, deep under the house, near the family tombs. It is cold and wet there."

"Let's go. My cough is not bad. Amontillado?"

"I hope so."

"It cannot be. And forget Luchesi. He does not know wine."

"If you say so."

Fortunato took my arm. I pulled my long, black coat around me, and hurried Fortunato to my home. Nobody noticed us. They were all enjoying the party.

There was nobody at my house. They were all at the party too.

They thought that I was away. They knew that they had to stay in the house. The day of the party was like every other day for my workers. That was what I told them. But they left the house, of course, after I left.

I took Fortunato through the house and down many, many stone steps. We were in the underground caves, with the tombs of my family, the Montresors.

Fortunato could not walk very fast. His eyes were wet and he did not look well.

"Where is the barrel?" he asked.

"Down there," I said, pointing in front of us.

He began to cough terribly.

"How long have you had your cough?" I asked.

He could not answer me for some minutes. "Do not worry," he said at last. "It is nothing."

"No. We must go back. It is dangerous to your health down here. Unlike me, you are a rich, important, and popular person. We will go back. I do not want your illness to become worse. I can talk to Luchesi about the Amontillado."

"Enough!" he said. "The cough is nothing. It will not kill me. I will not die of a cough."

"True, very true," I answered. "I did not want to worry you. But you should be careful. Here, have a drink of this strong wine. It will warm you."

I took a bottle of wine from the racks of bottles along the walls.

"Drink," I said, giving him the bottle.

"I will drink," he said, "to the dead people who are sleeping all around us."

"And I will drink to your long life."

Again, he took my arm, and we continued.

"These caves," he said, "go a long way."

"The Montresors," I answered, "were a big and important family. There are a lot of tombs."

"And what are those Latin words on every tomb? Do you know them?"

"Of course."

"What do they say?"

"Nobody can hurt me without punishment."

"Excellent!"

Fortunato's eyes lit up from the wine, and I felt warmer. We continued walking through the caves.

"It is getting too wet," I said. "We are below the river now. Come. We must go back before it is too late. Your cough will become worse."

"It is nothing," he said. "Let's continue. But first, give me another drink of wine."

I gave him another bottle. He drank all of it. Then he threw the bottle away and laughed. His eyes were burning. He almost fell. Again, I offered him my arm. He took it, and we continued walking.

Finally, we arrived at a large, deep cave in the rock. At the end of the big cave there was a smaller one. It was about one hundred and twenty centimeters deep, ninety centimeters wide, and two hundred centimeters high. It was very dark.

Fortunato tried to look in, but he could not see anything.

"Go in," I said. "The Amontillado is there."

Fortunato stepped slowly forward. I stayed right behind him. Then he reached the back wall of rock. He did not know what was happening.

There were metal rings in the rock, and I tied him to them in a second.

"My poor man," I said, "it is very wet and cold here. I will ask you again. Do you want to return with me. No? You cannot?

comfortable."

"The Amontillado!" he said. He was still unsure about what was happening to him.

"True," I answered, "the Amontillado."

From the larger cave I brought some tools and building stones, hidden earlier. I quickly began to build a wall in front of the smaller cave.

When I finished the first part of the wall, I heard a low cry. I stopped and listened. It was *not* the cry of a man who has drunk too much. Then Fortunato was silent for a long time. He was trying not to to show his fear.

I continued to work. Then I heard Fortunato trying to free himself. I stopped again and listened. When he stopped, I continued to work. Soon the wall was as high as my chest. Then I lifted my light over the wall so I could see him.

Suddenly, he began to scream. The screams were loud and strong, and I stepped back. I became afraid. Maybe someone can hear him, I thought. But then I felt the thick walls of the underground caves. Nobody could possibly hear.

I returned to the wall. When Fortunato screamed, I screamed too. My screams were louder and stronger, and he became quiet.

It was now midnight, and my job was nearly done. I only had to place one more heavy stone. I lifted the stone and began to put it in. But then I heard a terrible, low laugh. The hairs on my head stood up. Then I heard a sad voice. It did not sound like Fortunato. The voice said:

"Ha! ha! ha!—he! he! he! This is a very good joke, an excellent joke. Ha! ha! ha!—he! he! he! We will laugh about it often at your house when we are drinking wine together."

"The Amontillado," I said.

"He! he! he!—Yes, the Amontillado. But it is getting late. My

Suddenly, he began to scream.

wife, the Lady Fortunato, and other friends are waiting for me. Let's go now."

"Yes," I said. "Let's go."

"*Please, Monstresor! Please, don't!*"

"Why not?" I said.

I wanted him to answer me. I listened. I became impatient, and called loudly: "Fortunato!"

He did not answer. I called again: "Fortunato!"

Still he did not answer me. My heart became sick. It was too cold and wet underground. I quickly finished my job, and put the last stone in place.

For fifty years nobody has visited the tombs.

The Murders in the Rue Morgue

A strong man likes to use his body, but an intelligent man enjoys using his mind. He likes to solve *mysteries*. To ordinary people, intelligent people are often a mystery. Their skills can seem almost unnatural. One of these unusually intelligent people is my strange friend, Monsieur C. Auguste Dupin.★

In the spring and summer of 18—— I lived in Paris, and there I met Dupin. Dupin came from an excellent family, but he was now very poor. He had little interest in money. He lived simply. He loved books, though, and still bought many of them.

We first met at a small library in the Rue Montmartre,† when we were looking for the same book. We talked, and were interested in the same things. Then we met again and again. I was interested in Dupin's family history. He told me about it gladly, as Frenchmen often do.

Dupin was very intelligent, and he read many books. His mind was alive and fresh. I liked him very much, and he became a good friend to me. We decided to live together while I stayed in Paris.

Because I had no money problems, we lived in a large, old house. It was hidden away in an old part of Paris, called the Faubourg St. Germain.

We were very private, and saw no visitors. Our way of life was strange, but other people knew nothing about it and did not judge us. Dupin and I loved darkness and the night. During the day, we kept the house dark. We read, wrote, or talked. At night we walked the streets of the city, excited by its wild lights and shadows.

★ Monsieur: the French word for *Mr.*
† Rue: the French word for *street*.

Dupin was not an ordinary man. He could see things that others cannot see. To him, most people wore windows on their chests. He could see into people's hearts. Many times he told me my thoughts. He was a detective, but he was also an artist.

One evening, we were looking at the newspaper when we found a strange story. This is the story:

"MYSTERIOUS MURDERS—At about three o'clock this morning, the people of the neighborhood St. Roch woke up when they heard terrible screams. The screams came from the fourth story of a house in the Rue Morgue.

"The house belongs to Madame L'Espanaye and her daughter, Mademoiselle Camille L'Espanaye.★ Eight or ten neighbors entered the house, with two policemen. The cries stopped, but the people could hear two loud voices at the top of the house. These voices stopped when they reached the second story. Everything became very quiet.

"The police and neighbors began to search different rooms. The door to a large room on the fourth floor was locked, but they broke it down.

"They found the room in wild disorder. The furniture was broken. A bloody razor lay on a chair, and there was a lot of gray, bloody hair on the floor near the fireplace. Many expensive things and two bags of gold also lay on the floor. The desk in the room was open, but there were things still in it. There was a small metal box under the bed. It was open, but there were only letters and unimportant papers inside.

"Madame L'Espanaye was not there, but the dead body of her daughter was found in the chimney. The body was still warm. The face and neck were covered in blood.

★ Madame and Mademoiselle: French words for *Mrs.* and *Miss.*

"They found the room in wild disorder."

"The people searched the rest of the house, but they found nothing. Then they searched the small yard behind the building. Here they found the body of the old woman. Her neck was cut very badly. When someone tried to pick her up, her head fell off. Her body was also covered in blood.

"Nobody has been able to solve this mystery yet."

The next day's paper gave more information.

"THE TERRIBLE STORY OF THE RUE MORGUE— Many people were interviewed yesterday about the terrible murders. They are still a mystery. Below are the stories of the people who were interviewed.

"Pauline Duborg knew Madame L'Espanaye and her daughter for three years. She washed clothes for them, and they paid her very well. The two women were not only mother and daughter; they were also friends. Madame Duborg could not say how Madame L. earned her money. But Madame L. saved a lot of it. Madame Duborg never saw another person in the house. There was furniture only on the fourth story.

"Pierre Moreau sold cigarettes to Madame L. for almost four years. He was born in the same neighborhood, and he has always lived there. Madame L. and her daughter arrived at the house in the Rue Morgue six years ago. Monsieur Moreau saw the daughter only five or six times in those six years. The mother and daughter were very private. People thought that the ladies had a lot of money. Monsieur Moreau never saw another person go into the house, except for a doctor.

"Other neighbors told similar stories. Nobody visited the house often. It is not known if Madame L. and her daughter have any living relatives. The front windows of the house were almost never opened. The back windows were always closed, except the windows of the large back room on the fourth story. The house is not very old, and is in a good state.

"Isidore Muset is a policeman. He was called to the house at about three o'clock in the morning. He saw twenty or thirty people trying to get in, and he heard screams from inside the house. He broke the door open easily. The screams continued until the door was opened. Then they stopped suddenly. They seemed to be the screams of a person (or people) in great pain.

"The policeman went upstairs. On the first story he heard two loud and angry voices. One was low and rough. The other was high and very strange. The first voice was a Frenchman's. He heard the words '*mon Dieu*.'★ He was sure that it was not a woman's voice. The second voice was foreign; a man or a woman—Monsieur Muset was not sure. He could not hear the voice clearly. He believes that the language was Spanish. He described the room and the bodies as we described them yesterday.

"Henri Duval is a neighbor. He was one of the first people in the house. His story is similar to Muset's. But he thinks that the high voice was a woman's. He is sure that the speaker was Italian. He knew Madame L. and her daughter. He talked with both of them often. He is sure that the high voice was not Madame L.'s or her daughter's.

"——Odenheimer owns a restaurant. He comes from Amsterdam and cannot speak French. He was walking past the house when he heard screams. They were long and loud, and continued for about ten minutes. He was one of the people who went into the building. He believes that the high voice was a Frenchman's. But he could not hear any words clearly. They were loud but too fast. They were spoken by someone who was angry

★ *Mon Dieu*: French for *my God*.

29

and afraid. The other voice was rough, not high. It repeated, again and again, '*mon Dieu.*'

"Jules Mignaud works in the bank where Madame L'Espanaye kept her money. Madame L. owned some land and often put small amounts of money into the bank. She took no money out until three days before her death. At that time she took out a lot of money in gold. Another man from the bank carried the money to the house for her.

"Adolphe Le Bon is the man who took the gold to the house. Madame L. was with him. At the front door, Mademoiselle took one of the bags, and Madame took the other one. Monsieur Le Bon left. He did not see anyone in the street at that time. The street is often empty.

"William Bird is an Englishman. He went into the house, and he was one of the first people up the stairs. He heard the voices and the sound of people fighting. The rough voice was a Frenchman's. He heard clearly the words '*mon Dieu.*' The high voice was very loud—much louder than the rough one. He is sure that it was not the voice of an Englishman. It seemed to be the voice of a German woman, but he does not understand German.

"The door to the large room on the fourth story was locked from the inside. When people reached the door, everything was silent. They broke down the locked door only five minutes after they heard the loud voices. But there was nobody in the room. The windows were closed and locked. Every part of the house was carefully searched.

"Alfonso Garcio lives in the Rue Morgue. He comes from Spain. He went into the house, but he did not go upstairs. He was nervous. He also heard the voices. The rough voice was a Frenchman's, but he could not hear the words. He is sure that the high voice was an Englishman's. He does not understand the English language.

"Alberto Montani was one of the first people who went upstairs. He heard the voices. He thinks that the rough voice was a Frenchman's. He heard a few words. But he could not hear the words that were spoken in the high voice. He thinks that it was the voice of a Russian. He is Italian and has never spoken with a Russian.

"The chimneys of the rooms on the fourth floor are very narrow. Nobody can climb up them. Four or five men were needed to pull the body of Mademoiselle L'Espanaye out of the chimney. There is no back way out of the house.

"Paul Dumas is a doctor. He was called to the dead bodies in the early morning. The body of the young lady was black, blue, and bloody. There were deep red lines on her neck, made by fingers. Her face was a terrible color, and her eyeballs were very large. Her tongue was almost bitten into two parts. There was a large black and blue area on her stomach, made by a knee.

"The body of the mother was terribly cut and bloody. Her right arm and leg were broken. It seemed that she was hit by a very strong man with something very heavy. Her neck was cut with a very sharp knife.

"Alexandre Etienne is also a doctor. He was with Dr. Dumas when he viewed the bodies. He agrees with Dr. Dumas's opinions.

"This is an unusual murder and a great mystery. The police have little information and few ideas."

Dupin was very interested in the murders. "What do you think?" he asked me.

"I agree with the police and the newspaper," I said. "These murders are a mystery. I do not know how anyone can solve them."

"Do not judge these murders by the actions and reports of the police," said Dupin. "The Parisian police work hard, but they do not always see things clearly. They often look *too* closely. They make things too difficult. Sometimes, the true story is easily understood.

"So, why don't we try to solve these murders? It will be amusing. First, we will go to the house and look at it with our own eyes. I know G——, the Chief of Police. He will let us in."

We went to the Rue Morgue. We found the house easily, because many people were standing around it. They were looking up at the closed windows. Dupin looked at the street and the house very closely. I could see nothing important.

We knocked on the door and a policeman answered it.

"Your papers, please," he said.

We showed the policeman our papers, and he let us in.

We went upstairs to the room on the fourth floor. The bodies of the dead women were still there.

"Can you see anything unusual?" asked Dupin.

I saw nothing that was not described in the newspaper. Dupin looked closely at everything, even the bodies.

Then we went into the other rooms and into the yard. A policeman stayed with us all the time. We did not leave the house until dark. On our way home, Dupin stopped at a newspaper office.

Dupin said nothing about the murders until noon the next day. "Did you see anything strange in the house?" he asked me.

"No, nothing strange. Nothing more than we both read in the paper."

"The newspaper's opinions are not important. The police say that this mystery cannot be solved. It is too strange. But that is why we *can* solve it.

"First, the police do not know *why* the women were killed. Also, they cannot understand why two voices were heard upstairs. Nobody was, it seems, up there except the dead Mademoiselle

L'Espanaye. Then there is the other information: there was no exit; the room was in great disorder; the daughter's body was up the chimney; the old lady was attacked in a terrible way.

"The police believe that the problem is difficult. It is difficult because it is strange. But an ordinary answer lies *in* the unusual facts—not outside of them. In a mystery like this, we do not ask, 'What has happened?' We ask, 'What has happened that has never happened before?' So I have solved the mystery easily."

I looked at Dupin in silence. I could not believe what he said.

"I am now waiting," he continued, "for a person. Maybe he is not the person who killed the ladies. But I know that he was part of the crime. The man will come very soon. We will have to keep him here. I have guns. You know how to use one . . ."

I took a gun. I could not believe what I was hearing. Dupin was almost talking to himself. He looked at the wall as he continued with his story.

"People heard voices, but they were not the voices of the women. We know, then, that the mother did not kill her daughter and then herself. And we know too that Madame L'Espanaye was old and not strong enough. So someone murdered the ladies. The voices were the voices of the criminals. When you read the newspaper's descriptions of the voices, did you notice anything strange about them?"

"Everybody agreed that the rough voice belonged to a Frenchman," I said slowly. "But they disagreed about the high voice."

"You have not noticed the important fact. Yes, people disagreed about the voices, but that is not strange. It *is* strange that an Italian, an Englishman, a Spaniard, a Dutchman, and a Frenchman all heard the voice of a foreigner. And nobody could understand the language that was spoken.

"The voice was very unusual, but no words were heard clearly.

No sounds *like* words were heard clearly. That is why I can solve this mystery. But I will not tell you my thoughts yet. First, let's remember the room on the fourth floor of the house.

"Which question shall we try to answer first? How did the criminals leave the room? The criminals had to be in the room where Mademoiselle L'Espanaye was found. The police searched the house very well, and they found no secret doors. But I like to look at things with my own eyes. There were no secret doors—that is true. The door to the room was locked from the inside. The chimneys are too narrow for a person to climb. So the only possible exit was through the windows.

"There are two windows in the room, and both were closed from the inside with nails. The police could not open them. So they believed that nobody left through the windows. But *I* looked at the windows more closely. I believed that the criminals *did* leave through the windows. They could not close the windows behind them, so in some way the windows close themselves.

"I went to one window and took out the nail. It was very strong. I tried to open the window, but I could not. Then I knew that there must be a hidden spring in the window. I searched carefully and found it.

"So a person could close the window after he left through it. But, of course, he could not put back the nail. So I looked at the other window. It had a similar spring, and the nail in it seemed as strong as the other one. But I knew that there was something wrong with it. I took the nail out. It was broken in two pieces. One piece, though, was still in the window. I put the second piece of the nail back. Then I pressed the spring and opened the window. The first piece of the nail stayed in its place. But when the window was closed, the nail looked unbroken.

"So we know that the criminals escaped through the window.

The window closed behind him because of the spring. The window only stayed closed because of the spring, not because of the nail. The police did not look closely enough.

"The window, though, is on the fourth floor. So how did the criminals get down? A few feet from the window, there is a water pipe which goes to the ground. It does not seem possible that a man can reach the pipe from the window. The police thought so. But I was not thinking of a man. Think of the high voice that nobody could understand. Remember that no words were heard."

I began to understand. My friend continued.

"We know how the criminals got out. Let's think now about how they got in. The room was in disorder, but nothing important was taken. The gold was left in the room. The ladies were not murdered for their money. There seems to be no reason for their murder. The police cannot accept this, but I can.

"Now, let's think about the dead bodies. A woman was killed and put up a chimney. No ordinary criminal does something like that. And the criminal was very, very strong. Five men were needed to take the body out of the chimney. Hair was pulled from the women's heads. The old lady's head was almost cut off.

"So, think: a bloody, terrible crime for no reason; the wild disorder of the room; the strange, high voice. What do you believe?"

"A madman did this!"

"Not a bad guess. But think of the voice. Even madmen come from somewhere. Even madmen have voices that you can understand. And a madman's hair is not like *this*." In Dupin's hand was a piece of strange hair. "I found this," he said, "in Madame L'Espanaye's tightly closed hand."

"Dupin!" I said, excited. "This is not the hair of a person!"

"No, it is not. Please look at this book."

Dupin gave me a book . . .

Dupin gave me a book, open at the right page. I read a description of the East Indian orang-utan. These animals are large and very strong. They can act like people, but they are also very wild. Their hair is red and brown, like the hair that Dupin was holding in his hand.

Suddenly, I understood, but I could not believe it. "Dupin, you are saying that an orang-utan killed the ladies. But *two* voices were heard in the room. One was the voice of a Frenchman."

"True. And almost all of the people heard a Frenchman say '*mon Dieu!*' These are words of surprise or fear. A Frenchman *saw* the murder. But I do not think that he murdered anyone. I think that the orang-utan belonged to the Frenchman. It ran away from him. He followed it to the house, but he could not stop its wild actions. It is still free. But these are just guesses. And I do not like to guess. Soon we will know. Last night, when we stopped at the newspaper office, I put this note in the paper."

He gave me a copy of *Le Monde*. I read:

"CAUGHT—a very large orang-utan from Borneo. The owner (a sailor) can have the animal back. He must pay me a small amount for catching and keeping it. Come to number—— Rue ——, Faubourg St. Germain."

"How can you know that the man is a sailor?" I asked.

"I do not know, or I am not *sure*. But at the house, I found this hair-band. It could not belong to a woman. Sailors use this kind of band to tie their hair. Maybe I am wrong. But if I am right, the man will come here. He will not want to come. But he is probably poor and needs his orang-utan.

"He will be afraid, but he will still come. And why not? The police do not think that an animal killed the women. In fact, they know very little. They know nothing about the sailor. But *I* know about the sailor. And he does not know how *much* I know. So he will try to get his animal back. He will say that he lost it."

At that second, we heard someone on the stairs.

"Be ready with your gun," said Dupin. "But only use it if I tell you."

There was a knock on the door of the room.

"Come in," said Dupin, in a friendly voice.

A big, tall man came in. He had a sunburned face, a thick beard, and a long mustache. He looked very nervous. He was carrying a thick wooden stick. When he said "good evening" in French, he sounded Parisian.

"Sit down, my friend," said Dupin. "Have you come about the orang-utan? He is a very fine animal. I am sure that you can sell him for a lot of money. How old do you think he is?"

Dupin's friendly words were working. The sailor became calm.

"Probably about four or five years old," said the big man. "Do you have him here?"

"No, not here. He is in a safe place. You can get him in the morning."

"I am sorry that you have had to look after him, sir. I am happy to give you something for your trouble."

"That is very good of you. What can I ask for? Ah, I know. You will tell me everything about the murders in the Rue Morgue." Dupin said the last words very quietly.

As he spoke, he walked toward the door of the room. He locked it, and then he took a gun from his pocket. He calmly put it on the table.

The sailor's face went red and then very pale. He tried to stand and get his stick, but he fell back into his seat. He shook terribly. I felt sorry for him.

"My friend," said Dupin kindly, "do not be afraid. I promise that we will not hurt you. I know that you did not kill the ladies.

But you saw what happened. And if you are a good man, you will talk about it now. Tell us truly what happened."

"Yes," the sailor answered after a few seconds, "I *will* tell you. You will probably not believe me, but I will tell you. I will tell you because I have done nothing wrong."

He caught the orang-utan in Borneo, in the islands of the East Indies, and brought it back to Paris. He kept it locked in a closet. He wanted to sell it.

One night, he came home and found the orang-utan in his bedroom. It was holding his razor. The sailor was afraid and tried to calm the animal. But the orang-utan ran past him and out into the street.

The sailor followed it, but he could not catch it. He ran for hours. It was almost three o'clock in the morning, so the streets were very dark. Then the orang-utan saw a light coming from the house of Madame L'Espanaye.

It went behind the house, climbed the pipe, and jumped through the open window. The sailor was afraid for the people in the house. He knew that the animal was dangerous. He also climbed the pipe, but he could not reach the window. He could only look in, and watch.

The ladies were awake and were putting some papers in a metal box. They screamed when they saw the orang-utan. Their screams made the animal angry and afraid.

The orang-utan caught Madame L'Espanaye by her hair and cut off the hair with the razor. Then it cut her neck, and nearly cut off her head. When it saw the blood, it became even wilder. It turned to the younger woman, put its hands round her neck, and pressed hard.

Suddenly, the orang-utan turned and saw the sailor at the window with his stick. The Frenchman was screaming. The animal was afraid of the screams and of the Frenchman's stick. It

They screamed when they saw the orang-utan.

ran around, destroying the room. Then it threw Madame L'Espanaye out the window, and put her daughter up the chimney.

The sailor was very scared. He tried to calm the animal, but without success. So he climbed down the pipe and hurried home.

The Frenchman's shouts of fear were the words that were heard by the people on the stairs. The wild sounds came from the orang-utan. It escaped through the window before the police broke through the door.

There is not much more that I can add to this story. Later, the Frenchman caught the orang-utan and sold it. Dupin and I told the Chief of Police everything.

The mystery was solved, but the Chief was not happy. Dupin, as usual, proved he was a better detective than the police.

The Stolen Letter

On a dark, windy evening in Paris in the fall, my friend, C. Auguste Dupin, and I were sitting in Dupin's library, smoking pipes. We sat in the dark for an hour, thinking silently.

I was thinking about our earlier conversation on the subject of the Rue Morgue murders. I was surprised when Monsieur G——, the Chief of the Paris Police, suddenly walked into the room.

There were many things about Monsieur G—— that I disliked. But he was also amusing. It was a few years since our last meeting, so we welcomed him warmly. He wanted Dupin's opinion about an important matter.

"Can we have some light?" asked the Chief.

"If we need to think seriously," said Dupin, "it is better to think in the dark."

"You have a lot of strange ideas," said the Chief. (Anything was "strange" if the Chief could not understand it.)

"Very true," said Dupin. He then offered our visitor a pipe and a comfortable chair.

"What is the problem?" I asked the Chief. "Not another murder, I hope!"

"Oh, no, nothing like that. This is really very simple. I think that the police can solve the mystery without help. But Dupin will want to hear about it because it *is* very strange."

"Simple . . . *and* strange," said Dupin.

"Yes. That is the problem. The matter *is* simple, but we cannot solve it."

"Maybe the mystery is *too* easy," said Dupin.

The Chief laughed. "Oh Dupin, you *are* strange!"

"What exactly is the problem?" I asked.

"I will tell you," said the Chief, as he smoked his pipe slowly.

"But you must not tell anyone about it. If you do, I will probably lose my job."

"Continue," I said.

"Or don't," said Dupin.

"Someone," the Chief began, "has stolen a *very* important letter from the royal apartments. The thief is known to us. When he took it, he was seen. We know, too, that he still has the letter."

"How do you know?" asked Dupin.

"Because . . . things have . . . not happened. They *will* happen if the thief . . . uses the letter."

"Be clear," I said.

"Let's say that the letter offers its holder a . . . good position." The Chief was talking like a politician.

"I still do not understand," said Dupin.

"Hmm. If the letter is shown to a third person, an important person will look very bad. The thief knows this."

"So the thief *knows* that he was seen," I said. "He knows that the important person knows about his action. Who is brave enough to put himself in that position?"

"The thief is a government minister, Minister D———. Only he is brave and smart enough for this."

"Tell us how he did it," I said.

"While the important person was reading the letter in her bedroom, another important person suddenly came in. She did not want this person to see the letter. She tried to hide it in a drawer, but there was no time. So she had to leave the letter on a table.

"Then Minister D——— came into the room. He has eyes like a cat. He immediately noticed the letter, and he knew the handwriting on it. He saw that the woman looked worried and nervous. He guessed her secret. He talked and acted as usual, and took another letter out of his pocket. It was similar to the one on the table. He put this letter next to the one on the table and talked for another fifteen minutes. Then he picked up the other letter and left.

43

"She could not say anything because of the . . . other important person in the room."

"The owner of the letter clearly saw him do it. But she could not say anything because of the . . . other important person in the room."

"Ah," said Dupin to me. "So the thief really *does* know that the letter's owner knows about him."

"Yes," said the Chief. "And the thief is using the letter for his own dangerous purposes. The important person believes that she *must* get the letter back. But of course she must get it back secretly. She is very nervous about it, so she came to me."

"And who can think," said Dupin, "of a better person for the job?"

"You are too kind," said the Chief.

"It is clear," I said, "that the Minister still has the letter. While he has it, he is in a strong position. When he uses it, he will lose that position. And if he loses the letter, he will also lose that position."

"True," said G——. "And so I and the police have searched the Minister's rooms. He is often away at night. I have keys that will open every door in Paris. We searched his rooms every night for three months. *Three months*. If I find the letter, the owner will give me a lot of money. Do not tell anyone that, though. But we have found nothing. The thief is smarter than I am."

"Tell us about your search," I said.

"We worked slowly, and we searched everywhere. Each night we searched a different room of the building. First, we looked closely at and *in* all of the furniture. We opened every drawer. We searched for secret drawers too. Then we looked all around the building."

"Did you look through D——'s papers, and in his books?" I asked.

"Of course. We carefully opened every package, and looked at all of his papers. We looked through every book, page by page."

"Did you look under the floors?"

"Yes."

"Behind the walls?"

"We did."

"Then," I said, "the letter is *not* there, as you thought."

"I am afraid that you are right," said the Chief. "And now, Dupin, what can I do?"

"Search his rooms again."

"But I am sure that the letter is not there."

"That is all that I can tell you," said Dupin. "Do you have a description of the letter?"

"Of course!"

The Chief took a small notebook from his pocket and read a description of the letter to us. Soon after that, he left. He was not happy.

About a month later, the Chief visited us again. As before, Dupin and I were smoking pipes and sitting quietly. The Chief took a pipe and a chair, and began an ordinary conversation.

Finally, I said, "But G——, what happened with the stolen letter? Have you decided that you cannot catch the Minister?"

"We searched his rooms again, but found nothing. I knew that it was not there."

"How much money will you get if you find the letter?" asked Dupin.

"*A lot*. I don't want to say how much exactly. But if someone helps me to find the letter, I will give him a check for half of that amount."

Dupin opened a desk drawer, and took out a pen.

"Write me a check, please," he said. "When you sign it, I will give you the letter."

I could not believe it, and for some minutes the Chief did not move or speak. His mouth was open, and his eyes were wide. Then he quickly took Dupin's pen, and wrote a check. He signed it, and then gave it to Dupin.

Dupin looked at the check carefully, and put it in his pocket. Then he went to his writing desk and unlocked it. He took out a letter, and gave it to the Chief. The Chief held it in a shaking

The Chief held it in a shaking hand.

hand, and read it quickly. Then he ran from the room without saying a word. I never saw a happier man.

After he left, my friend explained the mystery.

"The Parisian police are usually very good," he began. "G——'s search was probably the best that was possible."

"The best that was possible?"

"Yes. They searched carefully, but their search did not fit the crime or the criminal. The Chief works hard, but he cannot think with a criminal's mind, only with his. That is enough for most criminals. The Chief knows how they think. He knows what they do. But if the criminal is very intelligent, the police cannot catch him. They have no imagination.

"For example, G—— and the police searched inside every piece of furniture. Only an *ordinary* man hides a letter inside furniture. But the Minister is not an ordinary man. He is very intelligent and brave. He knows how the police usually work.

"I believe that the Minister stayed away from his rooms at night. He *wanted* the police to search his rooms, and then to stop. He knew that the police only look for secret hiding places. So I believed that he used a *simple* hiding place. My idea was that the mystery was too easy. But the Chief laughed at this. Do you remember?"

"Yes," I said. "I remember it well. He laughed until he shook."

"The problem was too difficult for the Chief because it was too easy. Many people cannot see something which is obvious. The Minister knows that, and *I* know it.

"So one morning I put on a pair of dark glasses and went to the Minister's rooms. He was there.

"'Please excuse me, but I have to wear dark glasses because of my weak eyes,' I told him.

"With the glasses, I was able to look around the room while I talked to the Minister. He was sitting near a large writing table. I looked at it closely. On it were some letters, and books. But I saw nothing that was very interesting.

"Then I noticed a small letter rack. It was hanging from the shelf above the fireplace. In the rack were five or six visiting cards and a single letter. The letter looked old, dirty, and unimportant. It was addressed to the Minister in a woman's handwriting.

"I knew almost immediately that it was the stolen letter. It *seemed* different from the letter that the Chief described to us. It was *too* different. It was *too* dirty, and any visitor to the room could see it. The Minster *wanted* it to look unimportant.

"I continued to talk to the Minister in a friendly way. As we talked, I looked more closely at the letter. I saw that the outside of the envelope was really the inside. The address on the outside was new. Then I knew that it really was the stolen letter. I said goodbye to the Minister, and left. But I carefully forgot my hat.

"The next morning, I returned for my hat. The Minister and I began to continue our conversation from the day before. Suddenly, we heard a sound outside like a gunshot, and then screams and shouts.

"The Minister ran to the window. He opened it, and looked out. I stepped quickly and quietly to the letter rack, took out the letter, and put it in my pocket. In its place, I put one that looked similar. Then I went to the window. In the street, there was a man with a gun. Women and children were scared, but there was no real danger."

"How did you know that?" I asked.

"I know, because the man was working for me! The man was caught by the police. But he was freed because there was nothing in his gun."

"But why," I asked, "did you put a copy of the letter in the rack? You were in danger. Why didn't you simply take the letter on your first visit?"

"I stepped quickly and quietly to the letter rack . . ."

"I did not want the Minister to know that I took the letter. That was too dangerous. I wanted to stay alive. And I like the owner of the letter. For eighteen months the Minister has been able to do what he wants with her. Now, *she* can do what she wants with *him*.

"The Minister does not know that he does not have the letter now. But he will continue to act in the same way with her. He will destroy himself. Soon, the lady will not agree to his orders. Then he will open the letter. I would like to see him when he opens it."

"Why? Did you write something in it?"

"Of course! It was, I thought, the right thing to do. Once, in Vienna, D—— acted badly toward me. He knows that I will never forget it. He also knows my handwriting. So I wrote:

'My dear D——.
Your trick was brave. Mine was braver.
D——.' "

ACTIVITIES

The Fall of the House of Usher

Before you read

1 Look at the picture of the house on page 2. Describe it. What kind of people live there, do you think?

2 Find these words in your dictionary. They are all in the story.

crack (n)   grate (v)   melancholy   tomb

Which is a word for:

a a feeling?   **b** a hole?   **c** a place?   **d** a noise?

After you read

3 What happens after:
   a Madeline is put in the tomb?
   b the visitor runs away from the house?

4 Have an imaginary conversation.

Student A: You are Usher's friend. You have seen Usher and his sister and you are now talking to their doctor. How can you help the Ushers?

Student B: You are the family doctor. Talk about the Ushers' problems. Make suggestions.

The Maelström

Before you read

5 Answer the questions. Check the meanings of the words in *italics* in your dictionary.
   a What are *barrels* used for?
   b What does a *rainbow* look like?
   c What is another word for *sea*?
   d Where can you see the movement of *tides*?
   e Why is a *whirlpool* dangerous?

After you read

6 Why did the old man and his brothers go fishing near the Maelström? Why did they get into trouble?

7 Discuss the old man's feelings when he was in the whirlpool. Can you understand him?

The Barrel of Amontillado

Before you read

8 What do you do when someone hurts you with words or actions? What do you think a person in a Poe story does?

9 Answer questions about the words in *italics*.

    a Where can you find a *cave*?

    b What can you put in a *rack*?

After you read

10 Monstresor suggests many times to Fortunato that they can go back. Why do you think he does this?

11 Have a conversation.

    Student A: You are Fortunato. You want Monstresor to free you. Talk to him.

    Student B: You are Monstresor. You are going to put the last stone in the wall now. Answer Fortunato.

The Murders in the Rue Morgue

Before you read

12 "The Murders in the Rue Morgue" is a famous detective story. What usually happens in detective stories?

13 Find these words in your dictionary. Use them in the sentences.

chimney   nail   orang-utan   razor   spring

    a An . . . . . is a very large animal.

    b The smoke goes up the . . . . . .

    c I cut myself with my . . . . . .

    d You need wood and . . . . . to make a box.

    e I can feel the . . . . . in this old bed.

After you read

14 You are one of the people who went into the house after the "murders." Tell a newspaper reporter what happened.

15 The sailor says that he did nothing wrong. Dupin and the police agree with him. Do you? Why/why not?

The Stolen Letter

Before you read

16 Find these words in your dictionary:

drawer   minister   obvious   royal

Which word describes:

a a prince or princess?

b an important politician?

c a simple answer?

d part of a closet?

17 What are the possible problems when a letter is stolen?

After you read

18 Who do you think the letter is to? Who is it from? What is it about?

19 Have a conversation.

Student A: You are the Minister D———. You have found Dupin's letter and, a day later, you meet Dupin in a café. Tell him how you feel.

Student B: You are Dupin. Reply to the Minister.

Writing

20 You are Roderick Usher. Write a letter to your friend, asking him to visit you. Explain why you want him to come.

21 Write a description of a terrible storm. What was the storm like? How did you feel?

22 You are Monstresor. You are dying, and you suddenly feel bad about Fortunato's death. Write to Lady Fortunato. Tell her what happened.

23 You work for a newspaper. The murders of the Rue Morgue are now solved. Write a report.

Answers for the activities in this book are available from your local Pearson Education office or contact: Penguin Readers Marketing Department, Pearson Education, Edinburgh Gate, Harlow, Essex, CM20 2JE.